Who Wants a Dog?

To my children, Tom, Scott and Kelly Suzanne

Illustrated by Florine Porter

Who wants a dog?

Tom does not want a dog.

His little brother Scott does.

His little sister Kelly does too.

But Tom does not!

Scott wants a dog to play ball.

He will throw the ball; the dog will bring it back.

Kelly wants a dog to cuddle.

She will read a book with a dog by her side.

Tom does not want a dog!
Their family has never had a dog.
Tom warns his family:
"Dogs are always barking.
Dogs are always jumping up.
Dogs make messes. Dogs chew things.
Who wants a dog? Not me!"

Scott wants a dog. Kelly wants a dog.

Tom's mom and dad say they can go look at puppies!
Tom does not want to go. He does not want a dog!

They all hop in the car to go look at puppies.

There are two puppies in the pen.

One looks fluffy. One looks friendly.

Tom thinks the puppies are a tiny bit cute…

but they turn into…dogs!

And Tom knows:
"Dogs are always barking.
Dogs are always jumping up.
Dogs make messes. Dogs chew things.
Who wants a dog? Not me!"

They are picking out a puppy!

Scott wants the friendly pup.

Kelly wants the fluffy pup.

Mom and Dad ask the lady,

"Which puppy fits our family best?"

The lady smiles and says,

"Both puppies are special,
but this one is more playful.
He will run and chase a ball.
He will also cuddle."
Mom says,
"That's the one for us!"

Scott is excited!

Kelly is excited!

Mom and Dad are excited!

Tom is not!

Tom says,

"Who wants that puppy? Not me!"

The playful puppy comes home with Tom's family.

They name him Chocolate

Chip and guess what - the puppy is always barking!

The puppy is always jumping up!

He makes messes! He chews things!

And over time, the puppy grows up to be… a dog!

Life with a dog is different, just as Tom thought.

He sees Scott throw a ball, and Chip brings it right back.

He sees Kelly reading a book with Chip by her side.

Chip barks a little, but Tom knows that it's to protect them.
Chip jumps up because he is so happy to see them.
Chip doesn't make messes, and he only chews bones.
Chip spends his days outside playing with Scott
and inside cuddling with Kelly.

But at night when all is quiet and the stars are sparkling in the sky...

Chip is curled up, fast asleep right next to...

Tom!

Who wants a dog?

Me!

About the Author

Jan Ackmann MBA, M.Ed. Curriculum and Instruction, has taught Preschool and Kindergarten and through her work with preschool students, created a successful math and science enrichment curriculum known as Make-A-Mess. Jan is the founder of GAME-SET-MATH® (hands-on numbered balls and educational games), designed to teach important math concepts in Early Childhood Education. In addition, Jan has written children's literature based on her experience with young children. Who Wants a Dog? is J.K. Ackmann's first published children's book.